Entrepreneur & Kidney Donor,

Jeremy Colon

by Ben Gothard,

Founder & CEO of Gothard Enterprises LLC

Author of CEO at 20: A Little Book for Big Dreams

ISBN-13: **0997812494**

ISBN: **978-0997812497**

Project EGG

ENTREPRENEURS GATHERING FOR GROWTH

Project EGG is an elite network of entrepreneurs, authors & incredible people who problem solve, bounce ideas off of each other, share their stories and succeed together.

This mastermind includes people from around the world who are making a difference right now. We have a truly incredible group of people, like CEOs, CFOs, founders, national best-selling authors, inventors, marketers, coaches, consultants, musicians, speakers, and many many more entrepreneurs from every corner of the globe.

In the official Project EGG podcast, hosted by myself, Ben Gothard, different members of the group are interviewed. Each interview is a deep-dive into the life of the guest as both the guest and I drill down into entrepreneurship and personal development. By sharing their life and experiences, we can all learn something valuable.

This book is a transcription of the interview, unedited. Hopefully you can get as much out of the interview as I did hosting it!

Entrepreneur & Kidney Donor

Ben Gothard: Alright everybody, welcome to the first Project EGG interview. Today we're here with Jeremy Colon--a really, really cool guy. Why don't you introduce yourself real quick?

Jeremy Colon: Hey everybody, it's Jeremy Colon all the way from Boston, Massachusetts.

Ben: Alright, so let's kick this thing off. Jeremy, I just want to ask you as the first question: what is your story?

Jeremy: So what is my story? So a couple years ago, July 31st 2013, I underwent a kidney transplant surgery where I gave my father my kidney. He developed an unknown virus that was literally eating his kidney alive and ever since the--it's been about three years--ever since the kidney transplant, I was just more geared towards helping people out. I just have this feeling of or sensation that I just had help people in whatever way possible. At the time, I was pursuing being a personal trainer. After the surgery, I was a different person--like mind, body, and soul--I was clearly different. I felt different, I act different, and I was seeking things that will challenge me so I got into personal development, I got into reading a lot of books about life transformation, and ever since that I just ran with it and then I got into entrepreneurship and in my mind, I was thinking about what are the different ways I can help people for personal training. That's how I got into life coaching. 'Cause if I can not only understand people's mindset and understand where they wanna go, I can help them physically and make them feel better and transform their lives 'cause my philosophy is when you feel good, if you do good. With that being said, that basically just pushed me into other enterprises like social media marketing, being a social influencer. That pushed me into being a contributing author for a book and right now, the sky's the limit so I can just imagine what can happen in the next year or five years so I'm excited.

Ben: You were mentioning looking forward to the next five or ten years. But looking forward pretty far down the road, what is the most important thing that you want to accomplish in your lifetime?

Jeremy: The most important thing I want to accomplish in my lifetime is to give not only my family and my loved ones everything that they have sacrificed for me to be here. And for my family I want to give them a life of abundance and a lifestyle--I want to get them a life worth living because they sacrificed so much for me. I want to give it back to them tenfold. In my lifetime, I want to financially retire my parents. I want them to be happy. I want them not to stress with anything anymore. I want to wake up one day and just tell my parents, "stop what you're doing." I'm gonna call your job and tell them you're done, you quit. I wanna be able to walk to them and just tell them, your life is set for the rest of your life. Because what you did for me now, and all those years, I'm the person I am today 'cause of you guys. You guys pushed me so I wanna be able to deliver that to them. Aside from that, I also want in my lifetime to be the reason why people in the fitness world achieve their dreams and goals of having that body and feeling great. Not only physically peaked and mentally peaked, but spiritually peaked. Everything about your life is all-synchronistic where you wanna do more and you feel good about yourself. I wanna leave a legacy behind. One day I wanna have a picture on a wall with my face on it and have future generations look at it and say "I wanna be just like this guy that did it, he made it happen some way somehow."

Ben: Right, right. So you know you're talking a lot about legacy and leaving something behind. Whose legacy do you think was most impactful on you? Who's your biggest mentor?

Jeremy: My biggest mentor? Let me see. That's tough, because obviously I have more inspirations than mentors. I have intermediate mentors from personal development like Tony Robins, Jim Rome, Lest Brown, Bob Preacher. Those are my intermediate mentors - even Grant Cardone. I just trust their process, I trust in the coach. Every day I have my intermediate mentors: friends, family who pushed and support me. I consider everything they say valuable because they wanna go where I wanna go. They wanna dream what I wanna dream. The bigger the dream they have, the more challenging for people will be in the end. So in a way, it's like I learn from everybody. I'm not closed-minded to anybody who wants to talk to me, who wants to teach me a lesson. I'm like a sponge; I'm open to anything 'cause there's something about you that you can add value every day. Someone's out there who can add value to someone else. Whether it be you, whether it be someone in a group, whether it be my next-door neighbor or partner. Everybody has something to offer everybody.

Ben: You mentioned recently that you're getting big into entrepreneurship and you're authoring a big book. I know you just published that book. You wanna share a little bit about that?

Jeremy: Yeah, so the book is called Billion Dollar Success Stories and it's written with 42 other entrepreneurs from different career paths--from resume builders, to business consultants, finance planners, people who are once addicts who turned into serial entrepreneurs. The list goes on. But the book tells story about overcoming obstacles, what is our stepping stone, what basically pushed us to the brink were where we are now. Aside from the self-help books, where it's not coming from a millionaire point of view from someone who has achieved six figures, eight whatever. It's more for the common men so it's more relatable. It's really for someone who's working a 9 to 5 grind. State Street or Wall Street and wants to get out of it, but doesn't have the motivation or the mindset to really push him or herself to do his or her own thing. This whole book entails what the average person is doing. You don't have to be a well-known person to be successful. There's plenty of millionaires out there who no one even knows what their name is. That's what the book is, it's going to be part of a three-book series. We're gonna start probably planning for our next book in a couple of weeks. That's what it is, it's all

relatable. The whole mindset behind the book--
the whole focus on our book is adding value to
other people and instilling the vision that
anything is possible. You don't have to sacrifice
or do whatever everybody's doing; you can do
our own thing. You just believe in yourself,
believe that you can do and achieve it and it'll be
possible.

Ben: Right. How did you get into writing that
book? Like you said you were with 42--I believe-
-other entrepreneurs from around the world,
how did you get in contact with them, how did

you create the idea? Just give me a little background on that.

Jeremy: So The Billion Dollar Business Builders--that's the name of the group that contacted me. It was spearheaded by a guy named Travis Patterson and he just had this vision of putting up a platform that not only can fund businesses that people were looking for--gonna start a business, you need funding. A lot of people don't have the name or kind of barely have the resources to fund their business. A lot of it is out of their pockets. So the vision he had in his book was that for every book that people purchase, goes into a fund that can be given to people who qualify for a business funding. In a way, we are giving back to people who are really serious about their craft and really need it to get this going. Everyday there's someone out there who has the cure for something--has a cure or a solution--they have this innovation they just need funding and if you were given a chance-- we still have Shark Tank but not everybody can go to Shark Tank and get a loan--they have to give up a percent of the business. So this is a way for you to be an average person who wants to really make their life different and needs the funding, necessarily that we need to be.

Ben: This should be my second to the last question. If you could pass on one piece of advice to future generations, to other entrepreneurs, to other people who're trying to find success, what would that once piece of advice be?

Jeremy: I think the greatest advice that I could give anybody else--to the future generation is just be humble and be open to any opportunity, any bit of information, anything. 'Cause at the end of the day, we don't know everything. I can't walk in and tell someone, I'm gonna be a billionaire if I don't know how to get to that point in my life. So if I could be humble enough to ask someone or pay for their time and be patient along the way, then I can put a plan in place and it's about just being open to everything. Don't say no because you don't understand what it is. Say yes and learn how to do it later so that way you never know that bit of movement can get you somewhere you need to be. Just give it a chance and not being so closed-minded in the beginning.

Ben: That's great. And my last question before I let you go: is there anything I did not ask you about that you think is an important part of who you are as a person?

Jeremy: Let me see. Well, it would have been great if you asked me what type of books I read. Like I said, leaders are readers. I think what's helped me in my path to success and where I wanna be is honestly just picking up literature to read. Your mind is a muscle you gotta basically grow it. You gotta add to it every day. It's not just knowledge; it's applied knowledge. Read things that help you innovate, that inspire you, that build your creative mindset. I feel like a lot of people, I would say, probably 10% of the world reads a book, let alone get through a chapter. A lot of people just buy the book--don't pick up a book just to pick it. Read a book that's really innovative, read it a couple of times, highlight things that motivate you. Just like I said, go through it. Apply the practices and just apply it to your lifestyle and honestly see just where it goes. Give life a chance.

Ben: Absolutely. Alright Jeremy, well thank you very much for tuning in today.

Jeremy: Thank you, Ben.

Ben: You're the man. Everybody, this is Jeremy Colon from Massachusetts. Take care.

Jeremy: Thank you. Thank you, guys.